66

The Yasiel Puig Story

SportStars
Volume 3

66

The Yasiel Puig Story

SportStars
Volume 3

A Biography By
Christine Dzidrums

Creative Media Publishing

CREATIVE MEDIA, INC.
PO Box 6270
Whittier, California 90609-6270
United States of America

www.CREATIVEMEDIA.NET

Cover and Book design by Joseph Dzidrums
Cover photos by César Rivera

First Edition: July 2013

Library of Congress Control Number: 2013912516

ISBN 978-1-938438-30-1   10 9 8 7 6 5 4 3 2 1

For Joey,
My Favorite Dodger Fan

Table of Contents

"If you give the best of yourself, it doesn't matter what stadium you're in." – Yasiel Puig

TROUBLE

The Los Angeles Dodgers were in trouble. Basketball legend Magic Johnson and several other investors had recently purchased the historic team. After the very public sale, the club's new owners promised to restore the once winning baseball club to its glory days.

Yet the 2013 season was a disaster so far. After recovering from a shoulder injury, the Dodgers star player Matt Kemp strained his hamstring while chasing an opponent's double. Meanwhile shortstop Hanley Ramirez and left fielder Carl Crawford were also hurt.

The Dodgers' numerous injuries affected them greatly. The team with several World Series trophies now lingered in last place in the National League Western Division. Other teams in their division included: the San Francisco Giants, San Diego Padres, Colorado Rockies and Arizona Diamondbacks.

Dodger fans felt frustrated. Some expressed their disappointment by booing players during games. Others stopped visiting Dodger Stadium altogether. Management was desperate to make their fans happy again.

On June 2, 2013, Yasiel Puig sat in his tiny apartment in Chattanooga, Tennessee. The Cuban-born outfielder played for the Dodgers' Class AA club, the Lookouts. He led the team in many important stats: a .313 batting average, 8 home runs, 37 RBIs and 12 doubles.

Suddenly Yasiel's cell phone rang with news that every minor league player dreamed of receiving. The Los Angeles Dodgers were flying the 6'3", 245 pound athlete to sunny Southern California to play for their team.

A Dark Dodger Stadium
(Keadrick D. Washington / PR Photos)

Look out, Los Angeles! Number 66 was heading to the City of Angels. Puig-Mania was about to begin!

"The energy and talent [Yasiel] has, you can't duplicate that."
- A. J. Ellis

Chapter One

CUBA

Yasiel Puig was born in Cuba on December 7, 1990. Cuba is a poor communist country. Its government believes that resources should be distributed equally among its inhabitants. Unfortunately real life in Cuba is very rough on many of its people, many whom wish they had more freedom. Because the country is so close to the United States, its citizens often flee to America for a better life. Many want to pursue the American dream of working hard and reaping financial rewards.

On one winter day in Cuba, Omar and Maritza Puig were overjoyed with the birth of their baby boy. The couple named their child: Yasiel Puig Valdés. In Spanish naming customs, a person's name contains their given first name, followed by the father's surname and then the mother's surname.

Yasiel is Hebrew in origin. It means "Whom God made." The name is unique, even in Cuba. It's as rare and special as Yasiel himself!

When Yasiel was five years old, his younger sister Yaima was born. The family settled in Cienfuegos, a city on the Southern Coast of Cuba, where the parents worked as engineers. Cienfuegos is called Pearl of the South. The city's literal translation means "Hundred fires." It is a fitting name for the boy who would one day set Major League Baseball on fire!

Yasiel was a strong child who towered over other children on the baseball field. He always swung the bat with every muscle he could muster and smashed the ball with all his might. The youngster then sped around the bases faster than anyone. He could throw amazingly well, too. In short, he was a five-tool player, meaning he excelled at running, hitting, power, throwing and fielding.

Major League Baseball wasn't shown on television in Cuba but Yasiel still knew about famous teams, like the Los Angeles Dodgers and the New York Yankees. His country even aired the World Baseball Classic. The tournament features professional ball players representing their country of origin on national teams. The youngster loved watching the competition on television because it was his rare opportunity to watch big-league players in action.

Ichiro Suzuki: Yasiel's Hero
(Mark Dye / PR Photos)

Although Yasiel admired many athletes, he especially respected Japanese outfielder Ichiro Suzuki. The 2001 American League MVP was a phenomenal hitter and a constant threat to steal on the base paths. In 2004 he set Major League Baseball's record for most hits in a single season with 262. The formidable player also led Japan to two World Baseball Classic titles in 2006 and 2009.

Yasiel always eyed the World Baseball Classic with great interest. The confident teenager believed that he would one day play alongside some of the very players he watched.

Some people doubted that a young, unknown kid from Cuba could become a great Major League Baseball player, but the youth felt he could do anything if he set his mind to it. And when Yasiel Puig vowed to accomplish something remarkable, he usually did!

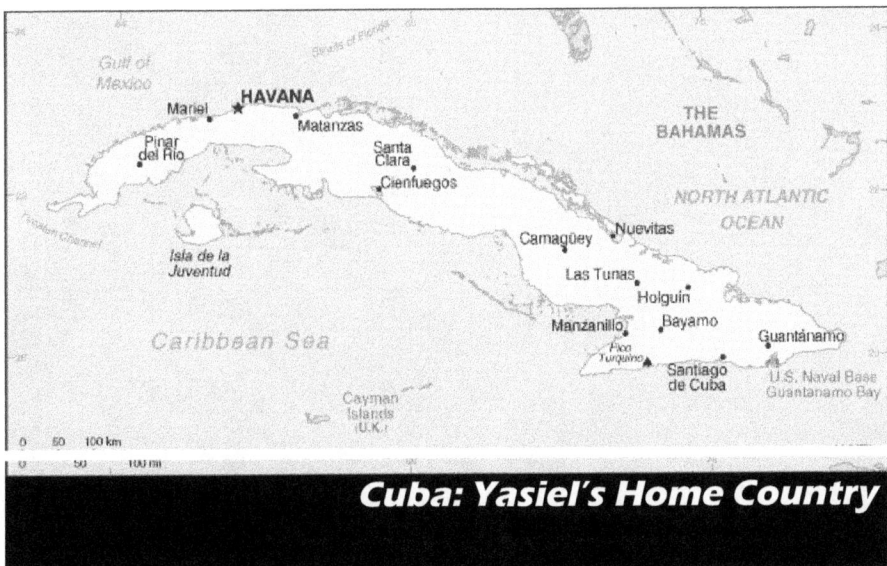

Cuba: Yasiel's Home Country

"There's an aggressiveness to the way [Puig] goes about playing baseball. He's up there with the intent to do damage." – Ted Lilly

Chapter Two

DEFECTION

When Yasiel reached his teen years, he began playing baseball on the Cuban National team. In July of 2008, the slugger and his teammates flew to Canada to compete at the World Junior Baseball Championship. While playing in Edmonton, Alberta, the seventeen-year-old realized how much he loved competing against other talented competitors and bonding with teammates. In the end, Cuba walked away from the competition with the bronze medal. South Korea won the championship, and the United States placed second.

Shortly after his 18th birthday, Yasiel joined the Cuban National Series. The amateur league consists of 16 teams, one for each province and two for Havana, with a West League and an East League. Yasiel played for his hometown team, the Cienfuegos Elephants. During every home game, he buttoned up his green and black #14 jersey and played ball in Cinco de Septiembre Stadium, a venue which holds up to 30,000 fans.

The excited teenager posted a respectable first season, hitting .276 with 5 home runs. The Elephants, struggled, though, finishing second to last in their league.

The youngster experienced a breakout 2009-10 season, notching an impressive .330 batting average, 17 home runs, 47 RBIs and 78 runs. His efforts led the Elephants to a second-place finish in the West League.

Meanwhile, Yasiel wasn't the only sportsperson in the Puig household. His sister Yaima competed in track and field's javelin throw. She won many medals throughout her career and could throw as far as 40 meters!

Although Yasiel earned a modest living as a Cuban ball player, he dreamed of playing Major League Baseball. How the youngster yearned to travel across America playing in fancy stadiums against the world's best athletes. It would be amazing to compete in playoff games or the World Series!

Except in order for Yasiel to compete in the big leagues, he would need to live in North America. Cubans were forbidden to leave their country without permission. If the teen wanted to play in the United States, he would have to defect from Cuba. Defect means leaving the country without permission.

Thousands of people attempt to defect from Cuba every year. Most Cubans pile into small boats with little food and water with hopes of landing safely in another country. People are often at sea for weeks. Some die during the dangerous mission, while many who survive are caught by the United States Coast Guard and returned to Cuba. Few actually succeed in making it to a new country.

In 2011, the Cuban national baseball team flew to Rotterdam, Netherlands, to play in the World Port Tournament. After Cuba earned a second place finish, Yasiel's teammate, Gerardo Concepción, defected from Cuba. The pitching ace established residency in Mexico, acquired an agent named Jaime Torres and signed a 5-million-dollar contract with the Chicago Cubs.

Yasiel still dreamed of playing Major League Baseball, too. He tried to defect from Cuba many times but was always caught and returned home. After one unsuccessful defection, angry officials banned the teenager from baseball for a year.

In June of 2012, the determined athlete finally defected from Cuba successfully. It was a long, painful ordeal which the player preferred not to talk about with reporters. Upon landing in Mexico, he established residency there and Major League Baseball declared him a free agent.

At last, Yasiel's dream seemed within reach. He was now eligible to play Major League Baseball!

Larger Crowds Awaited Yasiel
(Keadrick D. Washington / PR Photos)

"When you do the things he's doing, you create excitement."
- Don Mattingly

Chapter Three

THE SHOWCASE

While living in Mexico, Yasiel began working out rigorously. He also hired Concepción's agent, Jaime Torres, to represent him. The savvy businessman began drumming up interest in his newest client.

"There has not been a player as proven and as young to come to the States from Cuba," Torres said. "It's one thing to come to the United States at 19 or 20 years old with a few at-bats or some experience on a national level but this guy has years of national experience under his belt."

Major League Baseball teams typically acquire players through a draft system. Strong athletes are monitored in college, or even high school, before being selected in the First-Year Player Draft. Since Puig was from Cuba, scouts had to assess him differently. Torres invited teams to Mexico City to watch the young player.

Several teams who attended the showing expressed interest in signing Puig. The Chicago Cubs and the Chicago White Sox both wanted to add the player to their roster. One team outbid them both, though.

The Los Angeles Dodgers liked Yasiel Puig - a lot. Even though the club had only watched three of the Cuban's batting practices, they could sense his amazing potential. The celebrated team that brought the world Sandy Koufax, Fernando Valenzuela and Jackie Robinson wanted Yasiel to join their great legacy. They offered him a contract worth 42 million dollars for 7 years! He would receive 12 million dollars up front in a signing bonus.

"We feel that Yasiel can be an outstanding Major League player for the organization," Dodgers General Manager Ned Colletti remarked.

"Yasiel is a fantastic kid with an infectious personality and we think he has the tools to be a frontline player in the Major Leagues," said Dodgers Vice President of Amateur Scouting Logan White. "He is very physical and athletic with raw power. He can hit it a long way. On top of that, he has a good arm and is an above-average runner."

"Physically it was an easy call — he has the best tools of anybody I've ever scouted," White added to *The New York Times*.

Los Angeles Dodgers
(Glenn Harris / PR Photos)

Once the Dodgers signed Yasiel, they needed someone to help him assimilate to an American lifestyle. Those duties fell to Tim Bravo, a lifetime Dodgers fan who worked as the team's director of cultural assimilation. He specifically helped Central American players adjust to a new life in the United States.

The two men became fast friends. Bravo helped Yasiel open a checking account and find an apartment. They typically ate every meal together while the Cuban practiced his English skills. Yasiel trusted his new friend very much, called him "teacher" and considered him family.

When the caring athlete learned that Bravo's son suffered from cancer on his eyelid, he offered to pay for all of the treatments. The student's generous gesture brought the overwhelmed teacher to tears.

Yes, Yasiel Puig sure had a way of touching people. Soon he would ignite the entire city of Los Angeles.

Dodgers Dugout
(Glenn Harris / PR Photos)

"[Puig is] an energetic guy, eager to get on the field, loves the game and always has a smile on his face." – Adrian Gonzalez

Chapter Four

MINOR LEAGUE BASEBALL

In the summer of 2012, Yasiel officially began his professional career with the Los Angeles Dodgers. The team assigned the phenom to their Rookie league team, the Arizona League Dodgers.

"We're thrilled that Yasiel has arrived in Arizona," Logan White remarked to *MLB.com*. "He's athletic, intelligent and someone that's ready to work hard and earn a chance to fulfill his dream of playing Major League Baseball."

An initial designation to a Rookie league might have miffed some ball players but Yasiel handled it with the utmost class and dignity. The focused athlete felt determined to earn his way to the big leagues the old-fashioned way, with hard work and sweat.

"They can send me wherever they want," he told the *Los Angeles Times*. "This is all about me getting into shape, and if I don't get into the big leagues this year then maybe next year."

On Wednesday, August 1, 2012, Yasiel arrived at Scottsdale Stadium, home of the Arizona League Giants. In his American baseball debut, he was slated to hit fourth in the designated hitter role, when a hitter bats for the pitcher.

Unfortunately, Yasiel got off to a rocky start in his inaugural game. He went 0-4 at the plate. Meanwhile, the Dodgers fell to the Giants 5-1.

EXHIBITION GAME
STARTING LINEUPS –3/28/13

LOS ANGELES DODGERS

1 -	#25	CARL CRAWFORD	LF
2-	# 0	ALFREDO AMEZAGA	CF
3-	#6	JERRY HAIRSTON	RF
4-	#23	ADRIAN GONZALEZ	1B
5-	#47	LUIS CRUZ	SS
6-	#66	YASIEL PUIG	DH
7-	# 62	OMAR LUNA	2B
8-	# 81	MATT WALLACH	C
9-	# 93	BLADIMIR FRANCO	3B

STARTING PITCHER

#59	STEPHEN FIFE	RHP

RANCHO CUCAMONGA QUAKES

1 -	#6	DARNELL SWEENEY	2B
2-	#7	ERIC SMITH	C
3-	#18	COREY SEAGER	SS
4-	#22	ANGELO SONGCO	1B
5-	#23	JONATHAN GARCIA	RF
6-	#5	PAUL HOENECKE	3B
7-	#17	JEREMY RATHJEN	LF
8-	#24	SCOTT SCHEBLER	DH
9-	#19	JAMES BALDWIN	CF

STARTING PITCHER

#16	CHRIS REED	LHP

Spring Training Scrimmage Lineup Card

The following night, Yasiel was given the chance to show his impressive defensive skills when he played right field. He also found his groove at the plate. The slugger went 2-3 with an RBI triple and a blistering single.

As it turned out, Yasiel remained in Arizona for only nine games. The hot hitter was quickly promoted to a more difficult league after recording a scorching .400 batting average, 4 home runs and 11 RBIs.

Yasiel finished out the season with the Rancho Cucamonga Quakes in the Class A league. Playing in beautiful Southern California and wearing number eight on his uniform, he continued his strong hitting with a .327 batting average and 17 hits in 52 at-bats.

As fate would have it, Quakes manager Juan Bustabad was also Cuban-born. The skipper had arrived in America at the age of three and understood the trying cultural adjustments his newest player was going through. In regard to baseball, he greatly admired Yasiel's playing skills.

"He's got a lot of tools," Bustabad told Jim Alexander of *Press-Enterprise*. "He's got a plus arm. He's a plus runner. He has plus power. It's a matter of him now just playing games, getting experience as he plays more. Any time you take a year off and try to get back, it takes time."

Because Yasiel had missed a year of baseball after being suspended, his base-running skills were somewhat rusty. Dodgers staff members focused on sharpening the athlete's sliding technique and base-stealing mechanics.

When Yasiel was off the field, he continued taking English lessons. The Spanish-speaking player received instruction five days a week during the baseball season. With each passing day, the bright young man could speak and understand English better and better.

Rancho Cucamonga Epicenter
(Joseph Dzidrums)

One of Yasiel's favorite early memories in America occurred off the diamond. One evening following a game in Rancho Cucamonga, the stadium hosted a fireworks display. The kid from Cuba had never seen fireworks, so he stayed afterward to catch the event. His expressive face lit up in awe as he watched the aerial display in wonderment.

Soon the player would awe baseball fans with his own fireworks display on the baseball field.

Present & Past - Don Mattingly & Joe Torre
(Bruce Lemler / PR Photos)

"Puig's definitely brought an energy and a spark to us, and his skill level is more than anybody anticipated it would be."
- Stephen Fife

Chapter Five

PATIENCE

In 2013 Yasiel arrived in Glendale, Arizona, for spring training, determined to prove that he belonged in Major League Baseball. The talented phenom wound up producing one of the best preseason showings in baseball history with a staggering .526 batting average!

"I don't think I've seen anybody do something like this," Dodgers manager Don Mattingly raved. "You don't see this kind of package. This is a Bo Jackson-type package you just don't see."

"Puig is a talented player," teammate Carl Crawford raved to the *Press-Enterprise*. "He's got all the tools. He's strong, fast. He just looks like a Major League player."

Meanwhile Yasiel's parents and sister, who lived in a Florida home that the ball player purchased for them, traveled to Arizona to watch him play ball. The talented athlete felt ecstatic to be reunited with his family. Their presence helped ease his transition into his new American life.

"Everything is new to me, but I thank God my family is here," he told *ESPN*. "That makes me so happy."

When spring training ended, Yasiel believed he had proved he belonged in the big leagues, but Dodgers manager Don Mattingly called the upstart into his office for a difficult conversation. His skipper explained that although Yasiel had played extraordinarily well all preseason, the team simply didn't have space for him. The Dodgers already had three regular outfielders in Matt Kemp, Andre Ethier and Carl Crawford. The organization felt Yasiel would see more playing time in the minor leagues. He would begin the season at the club's Class AA team in Chattanooga, Tennessee.

Yasiel was very upset about his assignment. Yet he handled the disappointment like a gentleman and left the office quietly, vowing to make a big impact in the minors.

"I look at Yasiel as a Ferrari -- got the motor, the body, the wheels," Mattingly told *MLB.com.* "Just hasn't been painted yet and you don't want to leave it in the sun. We want a guy as ready as possible when he walks in the door at Dodger Stadium so he never has to go down again."

And so as the Dodgers top players traveled home to ritzy Los Angeles, a devastated Yasiel flew to Tennessee. As the club's cleanup hitter in Chattanooga, he accumulated 37 RBIs in just 40 games with a .313 batting average and 8 home runs.

As fate would have it, a few weeks after the regular season began, the Dodgers were suddenly in desperate need of another outfielder after Kemp and Crawford both went down with injuries. Fans began clamoring for the team to promote Yasiel to the big leagues with hope that he could help turn their losing season around. Suddenly the team was scrambling to get their top prospect on a plane and quick!

Yasiel Puig was finally going to play Major League Baseball.

Yasiel Puig: Los Angeles Dodger
(Jose Ybarra)

"I think he'll have a lot of flair. I think the fans in L.A. will like him."
- Logan White

Chapter Six

MAJOR LEAGUES

On June 3, 2013, Yasiel Puig arrived at Dodger Stadium. Wearing grey slacks and a striped v-neck sweater, the slugger smiled brightly as he slung his Dodger equipment bag over his brawny shoulders and headed straight to the clubhouse. He was now a Major League Baseball player.

As Yasiel unloaded his belongings into his polished blue locker, several well-known Dodgers walked over and welcomed him to the big leagues. His new teammates included an impressive All-Star roster. He would now play alongside 2011 Cy Young recipient Clayton Kershaw, three-time Gold Glove winner Adrian Gonzalez and two-time All-Star Andre Ethier.

Yasiel smiled upon receiving his freshly pressed uniform. The white jersey had blue cursive letters spelling out the word Los Angeles. The number 66 was etched in red stitching.

When Yasiel stepped on to the field for batting practice, he examined the enormous stadium surrounding him. One of Major Leagues Baseball's oldest and largest ballparks, Dodger Stadium held 56,000 fans. It had hosted many legendary events over the years, like Kirk Gibson's 1988 World Series home run and Sandy Koufax's three no-hitters.

Dodger hitting coach Mark McGwire greeted Yasiel with a bear hug. The baseball legend had broken Roger Maris' single-season home run record in 1998. Now he would help his new player adjust to Major League hitting.

After batting practice, Yasiel stretched his muscles in preparation for the game. He and good friend Luis Cruz spread out on Dodger Stadium's Santa Ana Bermuda grass and performed numerous warm-up exercises. They knew that stretching their muscles, tendons and ligaments before strenuous exercise decreased the chance of injuries.

Drawing a Cross
(Joseph Dzidrums)

Next Yasiel warmed up his arm by playing catch. He would start the game in right field, the same position he played in Chattanooga. Andre Ethier was shifted to center field and Scott Van Slyke would take the reins in left field.

Yasiel would bat first in the lineup. Teams usually position their fastest player in the leadoff spot so if he gets a hit or a walk, he will steal second or third base. Then the power hitters can drive them home with a big smash!

Moments later Yasiel and his teammates assembled on the third-base line for "The Star-Spangled Banner" which is played before every major sporting event. Yasiel removed his baseball cap to show respect for America's national anthem.

After the song ended, a large crowd cheered vigorously. The home-plate umpire called, "Play Ball!" and the Dodgers' newest rookie raced onto the baseball diamond.

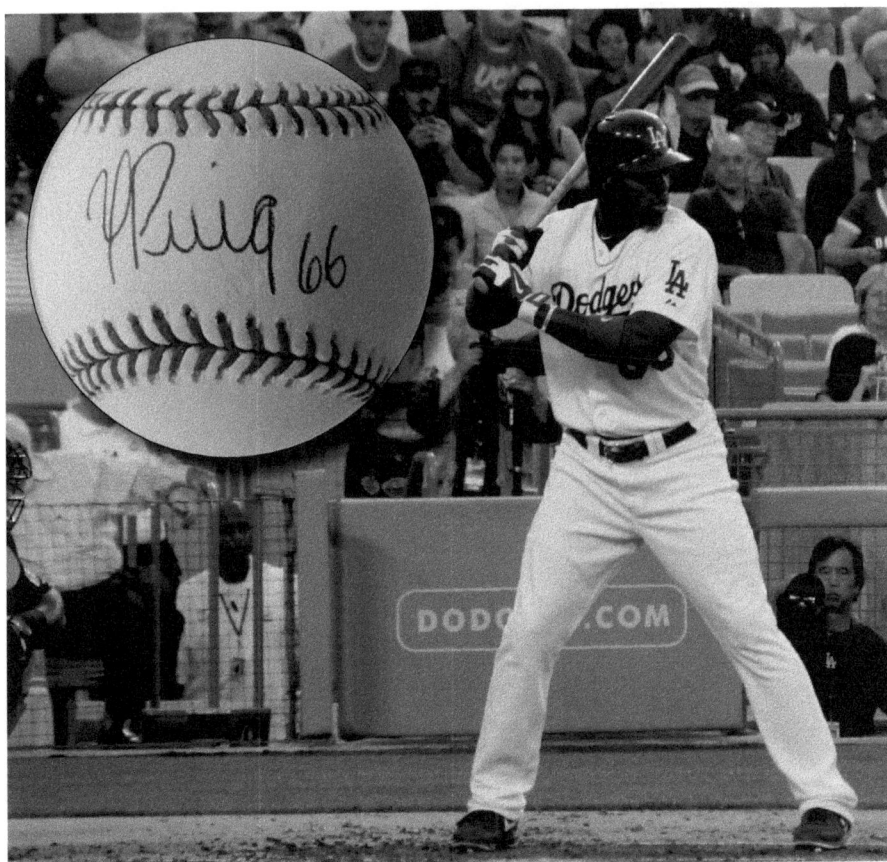

At Bat
(Joseph Dzidrums)

"I think everybody needs to see what this kid is doing because it's pretty amazing." - Matt Kemp

Chapter Seven

GAME ONE

Yasiel Puig stood on the on-deck circle swinging his wooden bat. The rookie eyed San Diego Padres pitcher Eric Stults as he finished warming up pitches. Meanwhile baseball fanatics watched Yasiel carefully. Some people even offered the new Dodger words of encouragement.

"Good luck, Puig," shouted one fan.

"Welcome to Los Angeles," yelled another.

Yasiel took a few more practice swings before he walked to the plate. The player used his bat to carve the sign of the cross in the dirt before stepping into the batter's box. He tapped his bat on home plate and assumed his regular batting stance. The upstart had an important job. As the lead`off hitter, he needed to find a way on base.

Stults first pitched a low fastball. Ball one.

The ace threw a strike next. When Yasiel swung and missed, fans groaned.

The newcomer reminded himself to remain patient. When the hurler's next pitch sailed high out of the strike zone, Yasiel kept his bat firmly on his shoulders.

The next pitch was better but he swung too late, fouling it down the third-base line.

On the fifth pitch, Yasiel timed his swing just right and looped the ball to left-center field. The crowd applauded the rookie's successful hitting debut.

"He got himself a Major League hit," Hall of Fame announcer Vin Scully exclaimed.

After reaching first base, Yasiel broke into a bashful grin. Third-base coach Tim Wallach signaled for the ball and tossed it to veteran Andre Ethier who stood in the dugout watching the proceedings. Yasiel now owned a nifty memento.

When the top of the ninth inning arrived, Yasiel had logged a successful first night, going 2-4 with two singles. The Dodgers led the Padres 2-1. Los Angeles needed just three outs to win the game. A victory would boost the team's morale.

Chatting with Juan Uribe
(Ron Reiring)

Dodgers' closer Brandon League retired the first batter but walked the second hitter, Chris Denorfia. The crowd grumbled in disgust. It had been a rough season so far for the team. Were the Dodgers about to blow another game?

With one out, Kyle Blanks promptly smacked a flyball to Yasiel. The strong fielder sprinted back to the warning track and nabbed the ball. Great catch! Suddenly Yasiel noticed that Denorfia had misjudged the ball and thought it was a hit. Now the player was frantically heading back to first base. The Dodger rookie fired a perfect throw to Adrian Gonzalez and nabbed him for a double play!

Randy Newman's classic song "I Love L.A." filled Dodger Stadium as the crowd roared in merriment. The enthusiastic fans showered Yasiel with a rousing standing ovation. He grinned sheepishly while celebrating with his teammates.

The Los Angeles Dodgers had won! Yasiel Puig was the hero of the game!

"I thank the fans for coming out and being here," he remarked to *USA Today*. "I'm very happy."

The Los Angeles Dodgers played their home games just minutes away from Hollywood film studios. Their emotional victory, led by their highly-touted rookie, seemed like a happy ending out of a feel-good sports movie.

"Really, with all the hype, it's just amazing it ends like that," Don Mattingly told *MLB.com*. "How can you not be surprised by that ending? You've seen games end like that, but not by a kid who's been hyped like him.

"This is Hollywood."

"Puig's on another planet."
– Clayton Kershaw

Chapter Eight

SUPERSTAR

Yasiel hit two home runs and drove in five runs in his second game. His first shot, a drive to left field, was so huge, it was the farthest home run hit in Dodger Stadium that season. As if to prove his versatility, the player hit his second smash to the opposite side of the stadium in right field!

I'm just happy to be here," a grateful Yasiel told the *Los Angeles Times*.

In Yasiel's fourth game the Dodgers were winning by a slim 1-0 lead when he came up to the plate with the bases loaded. On the very first pitch, the slugger smashed a home run over the right-field wall. A grand slam!

"I don't believe it," exclaimed Vin Scully.

As Yasiel rounded the bases, he pumped his fist triumphantly in celebration. Cameras cut to the Dodgers dugout where pitching ace Clayton Kershaw laughed and shook his head in disbelief. Meanwhile, the longtime Dodgers broadcaster had fallen silent.

"I have learned over the years that there comes a rare and precious moment where there is absolutely nothing better than silence – nothing better to be absolutely speechless to sum up a situation and that was the moment," Scully finally said.

By the time Yasiel reached the dugout, teammates bombarded him with congratulatory high fives. He and Dodger infielder Luis Cruz enjoyed a celebratory dance, while thousands of Angelenos demanded that their hero return to the field for a curtain call. All-Star Hanley Ramirez pushed the outfielder on to the field while the spectators roared their approval.

"I'm very happy with how things have gone for the team tonight," Yasiel said simply after the victory.

In Yasiel's fifth game, he hit another home run! By the end of his first week, he had received four curtain calls from Dodgers fans, who now seemingly chanted his name with regularity.

"I'm very happy that the fans are saying my name and the good thing is the team is winning right now," Yasiel told *MLB. com*.

Vin Scully had watched many legendary Dodgers players over the years. He'd called master games by fan favorites like Sandy Koufax, Fernando Valenzuela, Orel Hershiser, Jackie Robinson and Kirk Gibson. Yasiel Puig left him speechless.

"I've never seen a player who is a five-tool player show all five tools in three games," the revered broadcaster told *The New York Times*.

A few days later Yasiel's phone buzzed with a text. Before he could read the message, a second text came in - and then a third. Friends were texting congratulations. He had been named Major League Baseball's National Player of the Week.

The Cuban sensation had taken Major League Baseball by storm!

On the Road
(Garry Thompson)

"It's infectious the way [Puig] plays. There's a joy in his game."
- Don Mattingly

Chapter 9

SENSATION

Yasiel's popularity soared with each new day. He became so popular that the Dodgers produced a limited t-shirt in his honor, but they couldn't keep the item on shelves. The in-demand shirt always sold out on game days before the first pitch was even thrown!

Although Yasiel was the center of much attention and adoration, he didn't exactly embrace the spotlight. The player preferred privacy over the intense media glare. Before games he often lounged in the clubhouse dining room, where he knew reporters could not find him.

Likewise many players spend their time before a game researching the pitchers they will face. They examine recorded footage of the opposing pitcher so they can anticipate what kind of pitches he will throw. Yasiel shrugged off the pregame ritual.

"I just want to play," he told teammates.

And play Yasiel did! There appeared to be no one who played harder than Yasiel Puig. Whether he was firing a ball to a teammate, sliding into home plate, swinging at a fastball or racing around the bases, he played with all of his heart.

"A lot of folks pay good money to watch us play so we try to give them a good show," he explained. "We give our very best."

Now a full-blown Dodger, Yasiel had the fun opportunity to choose his own walk-up song, the music the stadium plays when a player goes up to bat. After deliberating through many selections, the rookie chose the Reggaeton number "Papa Dios Me Dijo" by Dominican-born artist Secreto al Famoso Biberon. The catchy tune's lyrics are a prayer to God, asking for protection from the evils in the world.

In mid-June the Dodgers flew to the East Coast to face their longtime rivals the New York Yankees. When Yasiel arrived in the Big Apple, he garnered attention wherever he went. Fans camped outside the Dodgers' hotel hoping for a glimpse of the slugger. Baseball enthusiasts packed Yankee Stadium to watch the sport's newest star in action.

Yasiel did not disappoint his many admirers. In a double-header showdown, the sensation went 4-9 with a home run, a double, 1 stolen base and 4 runs. In a fun twist, the home run he hit actually sailed over the head of his childhood idol Ichiro Suzuki! After the game, his hero had only praise for Yasiel.

"He's the type of player who makes an impact," Suzuki told *The New York Times*. "He seems like a fun player."

"You can recognize the tools right away," Yankees manager Joe Girardi gushed to the *The Canadian Press*. "There's an awful lot to like about this kid."

Although Yasiel enjoyed playing in Yankee Stadium and other famous venues, he especially cherished playing at Dodger Stadium. He felt chills when hearing fans chant his name. Enthusiastic cheers motivated him to play even harder and win more games.

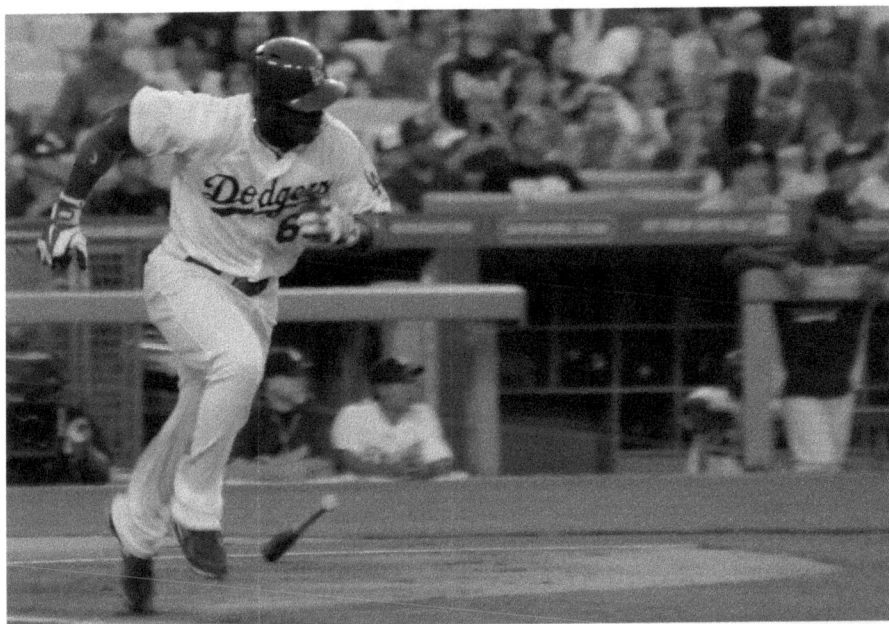

Running to First
(Joseph Dzidrums)

Yasiel fell in love with Los Angeles, too. Living in such a diverse metropolis ensured that he could always seek out his favorite comfort food. He found the city's best Cuban restaurants and frequented them regularly.

Playing team sports often leads to strong friendships. Yasiel became particularly close to Luis Cruz, the Dodgers Mexican-born shortstop who had a locker right next to him. Luis nicknamed the Dodgers' newest sensation: The Panther. Yasiel felt especially protective of his friend. Reporters, clamoring to interview the superstar after every game, often invaded Luis' space so much that he couldn't get dressed! Yasiel took matters into his own hands by using tape to mark a separation between his own locker and his teammate's.

"Don't invade Luis' space!" a thoughtful Yasiel wrote next to the line.

At the end of June, Yasiel wound up with more hits in the first month of his rookie year than any player since Joe DiMaggio in 1936. The Dodger ended the month with 44 hits, 5 doubles, 1 triple, 7 home runs and 4 stolen bases. He also posted a .436 batting average and a whopping .713 slugging percentage.

The popular Dodger racked up more honors when he snagged two awards on the same day, earning June's National League Player of the Month and Rookie of the Month. In addition, fans began a passionate, well-publicized campaign to get him elected to the 2013 All-Star Game. Because ballots were printed before Yasiel reached the big leagues, his name was not listed among the candidates. Regardless, he received a staggering 842,915 write-in votes.

Some baseball players who had played all year long expressed frustration that Yasiel, who had played about month, was gaining so much support. They felt the All-Star Game should feature a roster of players who had played all season. Yasiel shrugged off the controversy.

"Everyone is entitled to their opinion," he said. "It's ultimately up to the fans."

As a result of his strong write-in campaign, Yasiel became one of five finalists selected for the Final Vote, where fans vote for one last player to be named to the All-Star team. Dodgers fans rallied hard to get their star outfielder elected.

"Any athlete would like to be in the All-Star Game, but if I'm not selected, I would still be happy because my thing is for my team to win," Yasiel revealed to *USA Today*.

When the final results were counted, Yasiel just missed making the All-Star team. He placed second overall. Touched by the support, the player toured the Dodgers' offices thanking everyone who worked on his campaign.

"It makes me feel good to know that the entire organization supports me," he smiled.

Signing An Autograph
(Joseph Dzidrums)

Yasiel's gratitude extended to his fan base, too. Every home game, the number of supporters wearing #66 jerseys climbed higher. The grateful athlete always made time to sign autographs for his fans and pose for pictures.

In late June Yasiel was nominated for an ESPY Award, ESPN's annual sports award show. He would compete against other talented phenoms, like Seattle Seahawks' Russell Wilson, San Francisco 49ers' Colin Kaepernick, Texas A&M quarterback Johnny Manziel and Los Angeles Angels' Mike Trout.

Yasiel even learned that he had inspired a new rock band. Riley Breckenridge, drummer for the band Thrice, and Ian Miller, also a musician, are well-known baseball fans that run a baseball-oriented web blog entitled *Productive Outs*. The two men formed a new band entitled Puig Destroyers. The first single? "One Man, Five Tools."

Puig Destroyer
(Courtesy of Puig Destroyer)

Yasiel Puig's dream of playing professional ball in America had come true. He now traveled the country playing Major League Baseball. Children all over the world looked up to him and dreamed of becoming the next Puig. The popular athlete had won the hearts of sports fans everywhere.

Yasiel Puig was a Major League Baseball superstar!

Baseball Sensation
(Craig McCoach)

National League Rookie of the Month Award
(Joseph Dzidrums)

Essential Links

Yasiel Puig's Official Twitter Account
https://twitter.com/YasielPuig

Yasiel Puig's Official Instagram
http://instagram.com/puigyasiel/#

Yasiel Puig's Facebook Account
http://www.facebook.com/pages/Yasiel-Puig/188453287955327

Puig Destroyer Twitter Account
https://twitter.com/PuigDestroyer

Dodgers Official Web Site
http://dodgers.com

Official Major League Baseball Web Site
http://www.mlb.com

Puig-Mania
(Joseph Dzidrums)

Christine Dzidrums has written biographies on many inspirational figures: Matt Kemp, Mike Trout, Yasiel Puig, Clayton Kershaw, Joannie Rochette, Yuna Kim, Shawn Johnson, Nastia Liukin, The Fierce Five, Gabby Douglas, Sutton Foster, Kelly Clarkson, Idina Menzel and Missy Franklin.

Christine's fictional works include: *Cutters Don't Cry,* (Moonbeam Children's Book Award), *Fair Youth, Timmy and the Baseball Birthday Party, Timmy Adopts a Girl Dog, Future Presidents Club* and *Princess Dessabelle Makes a Friend.*

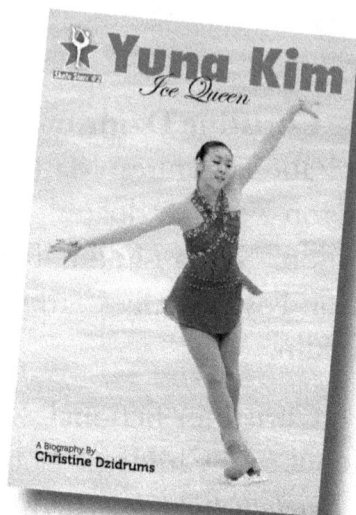

At the 2010 Vancouver Olympics, tragic circumstances thrust **Joannie Rochette** into the spotlight when her mother died two days before the ladies short program. Joannie then captured hearts everywhere by courageously skating two moving programs to win the Olympic bronze medal.

Joannie Rochette: Canadian Ice Princess profiles the popular figure skater's moving journey.

Meet figure skating's biggest star: **Yuna Kim**. The Korean trailblazer produced two legendary performances at the 2010 Vancouver Olympic Games to win the gold medal. *Yuna Kim: Ice Queen* uncovers the compelling story of how the beloved figure skater overcame poor training conditions, various injuries and numerous other obstacles to become world and Olympic champion.

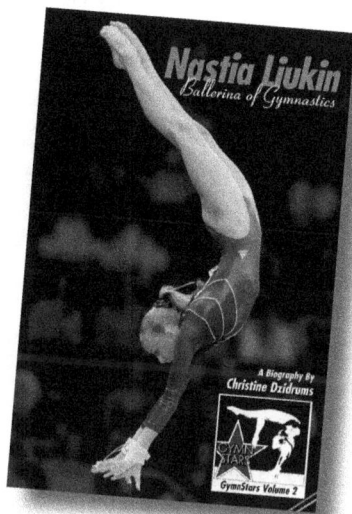

Shawn Johnson, the young woman from Des Moines, Iowa, captivated the world at the 2008 Beijing Olympics when she snagged a gold medal on the balance beam.

Shawn Johnson: Gymnastics' Golden Girl, the first volume in the **GymnStars** series, chronicles the life and career of one of sports' most beloved athletes.

Widely considered America's greatest gymnast ever, **Nastia Liukin** has inspired an entire generation with her brilliant technique, remarkable sportsmanship and unparalleled artistry.

A children's biography, *Nastia Liukin: Ballerina of Gymnastics* traces the Olympic all-around champion's ascent from gifted child prodigy to queen of her sport.

Also From

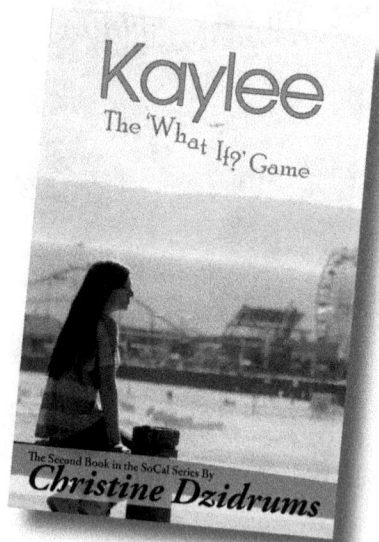

2010 Moonbeam Children's Book Award Winner! In a series of raw journal entries written to her absentee father, a teenager chronicles her penchant for self-harm, a serious struggle with depression and an inability to vocally express her feelings.

"I play the 'What If?'" game all the time. It's a cruel, wicked game."

When free spirit Kaylee suffers a devastating loss, her personality turns dark as she struggles with depression and unresolved anger. Can Kaylee repair her broken spirit, or will she remain a changed person?

Creative Media Publishing

Princess Dessabelle
Makes a Friend

Written By
Christine Dzidrums

Illustrated By
Tohn Fayette Müths

Meet **Princess Dessabelle**, a spoiled, lonely princess with a quick temper. When she orders a kind classmate to be her friend, she learns the true meaning of friendship.

Build Your Timmy™
Collection Today!

Meet Timmy Martin, the world's biggest baseball fan.

One day the young boy gets invited to his cousin's birthday party. Only it's not just any old birthday party... It's a baseball birthday party!

Timmy and the Baseball Birthday Party is the first book in a series of stories featuring the world's most curious little boy!

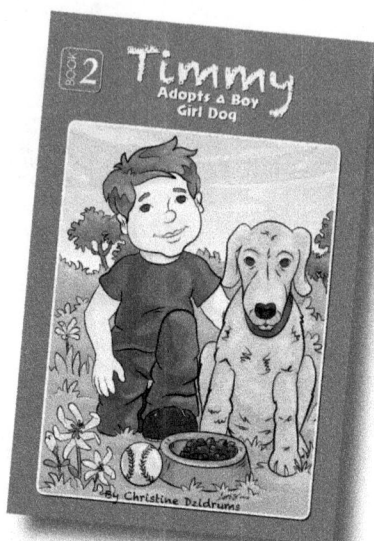

Timmy Martin has always wanted a dog. Imagine his excitement when his mom and dad let him adopt a pet from the animal shelter. Will Timmy find the perfect dog? And will his new pet know how to play baseball?

Timmy Adopts A Girl Dog is the second story in the series about the world's most curious 4½ year old.

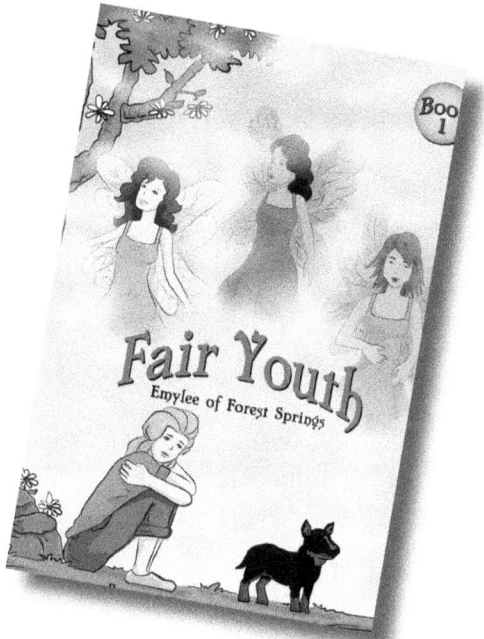

Twelve-year-old Emylee Markette feels invisible. Then one fateful afternoon, three beautiful sisters arrive in her sleepy New England town and instantly become the most popular girls at Forest Springs Middle School. To everyone's surprise, the Fay sisters befriend Emylee and welcome her into their close-knit circle.

Through it all, though, Emylee's weighed down by nagging suspicions. Why were the Fay sisters so anxious to befriend her? How do they know some of her inner thoughts? What do they truly want from her?

When Emylee eventually discovers that her new friends are secretly fairies, she finds her life turned upside down yet again and must make some life-changing decisions.

Fair Youth: Emylee of Forest Springs is the first book in an exciting new series for tweens!